CHRIS NEALON

# THE SHORE

WAVE BOOKS    SEATTLE / NEW YORK

Published by Wave Books

www.wavepoetry.com

Copyright © 2020 by Chris Nealon

Wave Books titles are distributed to the trade by

Consortium Book Sales and Distribution

Phone: 800-283-3572 / SAN 631-760X

Library of Congress Cataloging-in-Publication Data

Names: Nealon, Christopher S. (Christopher Shaun), 1967– author.

Title: The shore / Chris Nealon.

Description: First edition. | Seattle : Wave Books, [2020]

Identifiers: LCCN 2019030060

ISBN 9781940696973 (trade paperback)

ISBN 9781940696980

Classification: LCC PS3614.E247 A6 2020 | DDC 811/.6—dc23

LC record available at https://lccn.loc.gov/2019030060

Designed by Crisis

Printed in the United States of America

9 8 7 6 5 4 3 2 1

First Edition

Wave Books 084

FOR NICO

# THE VICTORIOUS ONES

1

Then came fire

We drove out past the flooding to watch the birds

Long-lashed boys in hoodies looked up from the sidewalk to absorb
   the sky

Ancient women left the bedsides of their long-ago boys

And in the great transition no one could tell if we were doomed or free

2

Is there an original exile?

I think the Germans think we were driven from the forest

Sometimes like a distant station playing a tune you half-remember I
    can hear it—

        Driven out into the terrifying open        to savanna

That's not my myth

Or, I don't want it to be

# 3

I do like imagining high-value objects become nearly worthless
People just leaving their prized possessions lying around

It gives me a rest from that squirrelly huddling near the outlets feeling
That well if a catastrophe hits at least my phone will be charged idea

So maybe just leave it on the toilet for the next guy
Maybe just delete all your contacts and go

# 4

My friends encourage me, take care of me

"You should totally become an anarchist! Just stay off the listserv."

I was deep in the kaleidoscope,

Feeling it allowing me to sense all time, but I couldn't tell anyone
about it—

Perhaps because I was dead

# 5

A daylit surface teeming with youth—it makes me feel like mine has
been—not lost so much as just . . . subducted

Abruptly it's the final day of spring—

      Your pointillist relationship to calendar time
      Tap that date / tap that date / tap it

      Touchscreen indifferent to your bandaged thumb

And yes like every other poet with a child I have dreamed of mine
along some empty road in camouflage and tatters, scrambling for
potable water in 2046

But you know what? Fuck the zombie apocalypse

I'm going to imagine him with comrades

# 6

Oh man praying to the wrong gods again

    Please flux keep me open    just another poem

    Whoops no see you later

Thirteen weeks of winter salt across the Al Jazeera banner

April lawns and trees Chaucerian and raggedy with hungry geese
    and mockingbirds

We were sold kenosis as a way to overcome discrepancies in scale

But everything hinged on the tone you did it in

# 7

There's a river running backward through this poem to the sources
    of literature

You'd think that would be a good thing

But I take seriously that beauty is the beginning of terror, in a
    quarreling way

I do think beauty halfway staves off terror with forms, with dance,
    with symbols,

      And I know we're never far from terror—

But here's the thing: even saying that sounds right-wing

And that's because the right has always practiced terror to insist that
    we can never get away from it

      I say this as a homosexual

Terror—that's the meaning of male homophobia—

It's not a fear of buttfucking, please—it's the punishment of male
   insouciance, male lightness, a bodily comportment and a vocal
   inflection that gets heard as

   *everything is beautiful*     *everything is fine*

Those hammerblows administered to gay boys' skulls—they say
   NO—we are *not* free from violence—this is not Arcadia—how
   dare you flounce around—

So when my colleagues critique The Romantic Symbol, critique the
   Romantics, for peddling false consolation—

When the modernists champion objectivity, and unsymbolizable
   allegory,

      Because we know better than to trust in pretty symbols but
         keep forgetting,

      Because we need art to remind us that life is hard,

         I wonder—

Who are we talking to? I mean three cheers for allegory

But there's a gossamer, a hollow way of symbols, isn't there

There's a way a beaten body looks in silk

> I didn't become a professor so I could "demystify" my
> students

> I didn't kiss that boy in 1987 because I'd forgotten terror

Maybe Rilke writing on the dime of the House of Thurn and Taxis
knew this

Maybe he didn't just mean, whoa, those angels are *intense*

Either way when I say "beauty" I don't mean razzle-dazzle, and I don't
mean the crucifixion

> When I say "terror" I don't mean the Titans

There's a river running backward through this poem to the sources of
our struggle with each other

## 8

Guilty as charged!
I do have something to peddle

But you know I can't help it—I came of age in the great mixtape
    swap meet of the 1980s—

       Hey, you want to feel like this?
       Hey, I have a crush on you, put this in your pocket

Later watching waters part around my friend—since gone on to
    glory—as he took over the club

As though the early 90s were an apical moment in the history of
    longing—

As though those vocals, Robin S, had hit a plaintive note that was
    not to be repeated—

When in fact it was just another episode of black women teaching
    white boys how to ache for free

# 9

Later still—a Saturn return—

Me and Stephen on the Schäfergasse, chatting up the barback on a
   strangely silent Friday night

   "Hey, where *are* the gay people in Frankfurt, anyway?"
   "Oh, they are in the forest . . ."

# 10

So yeah the mythic method

"This place Hammertown I'm talking about, this imaginary place, actually has a very, very specific history . . . a history of genocide. And that's something that the poetics I am proposing has absolutely no way of dealing with. There are a lot of reasons why I stopped but that's certainly one of them . . . It's just an aspect of that reality that I was never going to be able to deal with."

# 11

Peter Culley I thought you should know—

The day after you died I took *Parkway* with me into the woods

    Or, well . . . it was Rock Creek Park

I fell asleep contentedly beneath a tree, around the halfway point—

I wasn't dreaming quite—my sleep was not that deep—

But in the quiet I could hear you approach

I heard you telling me that you'd liked reading backward, as a child

I felt you were describing, in case I wanted to try it, how you'd
    learned to write those lines like brushed-up nap on a trampled
    carpet, fresh again—

    You know I'll never have your mad skills

But I'm taking you with me into the woods

# 12

Peter I bet you knew this let-down post-revolutionary feeling—

This lower-limit-private-perception feeling

This too-too-solid flesh / hell is other people / Artaudian
hell is my body feeling

Most days these days I've got nothing but my tepid intellectual
watchfulness

But sometimes in distraction I get tugged at from behind—tugged at
from within this chidākāsha backdoor in the mind

I usually ignore it but every now and then I turn the handle and it's
like BAM—

A Narnia of forms!

Insubstantial forms—

Peter this is better

It's as though the ache in me to find substantiality subsides—

The ache to find it in boys' bodies—to find it in the firmest earth on
which to take a stand

That firm ground would never be enough against the weapon they have
stashed in readiness against us—

Those hammerblows—

Those who-do-you-think-you-are letters from the FBI urging
revolutionaries to consider suicide—

But we're unjustified

It's like the sword thrust into us would just find . . . nothing

Like we know our poetry's as nothing to the waves of sound

# 13

So yeah I watched a lot of space epics as a kid

Look at me, all Obi-Wan

But fantasies aren't just implanted in us—they tap into something,
right?

Trembling        inexistent

Poets—sometimes I am proud of us—

How a stanza is a woofer pulsing—

How wood to us is beautiful but also an impedance

# 14

Your private perceptions—

Clarity—November like a wrung sponge—

Your eye hops over from the dissipated contrail to the crisp one and
then tracks southward to the actual plane

Mental recapitulation of the sensuous world—like I had an ice-hand
that could freeze the tip of every branch—

Ice world, white forest—

Held in some salinity—some meter—

# 15

Courage like cool water

We sat on a bank and read from the always-only deuterocanonical
    books we loved

We made a dossier of terrifying descriptions of the sky and bound
    the sheaves together with red thread

And we came back to that scene in *The Salt Eaters* where the Sisters
of the Yam are headed to a demonstration, traveling dirt roads in
rural Georgia on a rickety old bus, when they look up, all twelve of
them, and something in the pivot of a flock of birds makes them
realize that the roof of time has been torn off

    "Tendon, feather, bone and flesh were riding against a
backdrop of eight-minute-ago blue, of fifty-years-ago blue,
rode the curvature to the seam . . ."

How I pray for access to that feeling!

        Toni Cade Bambara       you are missed

# 16

So look I know I won't see the end of capital

But you, child—I wonder—

Surely it won't be pretty

    Yes I know    protective gear    awkward alternative currencies

But maybe also how it might be said of you / that you were the ones
    who saw it through

        The destruction from below of all the fucked-up supply chains
            by those giant worms from Dune

        The dropping like a fly of every drone

I've seen you by the window with your beautiful wide eyes as storms
    rolled in

        I've tried to teach you the words

I've imagined you remembered at the end of a long life, circled by
friends beneath an empty sky,

Your friends who wrote the poems of the 22nd century,

The poems of storms and drones,

And hoped that when they reached the line about you it would
read,

*He who loved lightning watched them fall*

# 17

Then came fire

It wasn't yet a new world, or the end of the old one

But water, money, feeling overspilled their banks

There was finally something real to be afraid of

There was finally no reason to fear

Even animals approached us as they hadn't in ten thousand years

Buildings were either shelter or they weren't

Music got quiet

And poetry—

Poetry began to ask the question it had hidden in the forest

Poetry returned to lists, enumeration, inventory

It chose sides

This was not the same as prophecy

Look around you now      and ask yourself

Which of these—

      The innovators, profit-makers, the ones behind high walls,

            The ones who are planning for the great catastrophes—

      Or the ones with no ability to plan,

      Who live from hour to hour, year to year,

            In whom terror waits to be uncurdled,

      Who live in the great wide world—

Which of these will be the victorious ones?

Nobody knows.

YOU SURROUND ME

Let's say you have a sexual fantasy that makes you feel like a man.

Say it makes the chi run down your body in separate streams until it
  crosses at the groin—become a V—become an X—

Shyly at first along the distal extremes then rushing past itself in
  heedlessness half joy and half exasperation

Reverb: music of the spheres as you approached your $VO_2$ Max

Afterimage: uncrossed wires giving scorched and vivid outline to your
  body

    So now you feel like a man

But what on earth is a man?

    *


A little bit cis / a little bit trans

    Alpine terms for matters subterranean—

Transpadania / Cispadania—French then briefly Austrian in the spring
of 1799—

Napoleon was really trying everything in the run-up to empire

Then the indeterminate polity for which there was no better name than
"League"—

The League of God's House / League of the Ten Jurisdictions

Oh hell, the Bishopric of Chur—

Of course this is the internet talking

But it's also my body

Cadence is my body talking

And you—how you confuse me with your rolling gait—

Crossing leagues to reach you on the other side of the room—

        *

The knot in your body you call desire is not the truth, it's a
    commitment—made unheeding, made too early—

    And even when it's phallic it's defensive

    It loosens shyly in arousal then retightens

Tuning in to graceful carriage always makes me feel bisexual—

        A little mystical—

Then I crash to earth

You can have sex only with men, but it's not like homotopia is
    patriarchy-free

You can have sex just with white boys, but, mm, that's sort of the
    problem

There's a dialogue I tumble into during orgasm, it goes

    What do you know about people's souls?

    Hardly anything

    *

Standing over the little bed where Keats died—thinking of that Oppen
poem—

    "A friend saw the rooms
    Of Keats and Shelley
    At the lake, and saw 'they were just
    Boys' rooms' and was moved

    By that..."

Keats's senses—they surrounded him—world-suffused and
bursting—full of breezes

    And next in fullness to the dark—

Like he felt he had to be hollow to take in the world

    Later in my own bed—

Open window—gibbous moon—the pulse of jasmine and the evening
cries of seagulls—

And another scent beneath it all—the half-life scent construction
leaves—ceramic tile and cedar planks and fabric and lacquer—

The scent I bet makes those who grew up with it miss it when they
    travel, though they never sense it when they're home—

        The deciduous wave that hit me in Ithaca

        Or the scent I came to know in Barcelona, pervading
            everything,
        down to birdsong—

        Mediterranean

Salt that opens deep interiors—

        A depth like "quiet breathing" that means, not volumetric but
            suffusing—

        And your spirographic movement through it—

That surround—not what they call Switzerland, not what they call
    Rome—

That was where he lived


        *

And who are you?

You're every boy I ever—

No . . . you're more than that—you're Michael Tolliver in 1975,
    telling Mary Ann he fell in love three times today on the bus ride
    home—

You're Mary Ann—

Or—I don't know—I'm just not sure how wide my soul can go—I
    can't be Whitman—

Though maybe from another angle—

I can't see vistas but I sense interstices—

*

To feel surrounded—to be shot through—

Freud called it paranoia: fear that all the labor of the making of your
    unitary body could be undone

Undone by the river of desire—"river" here in general meaning
    homosexuality—

    That was 1922

By 1968 Guy Hocquenghem is having none of it—homosexuals
    aren't paranoid, queerness is *relief* from paranoia—from the fear
    of not being normal,

    It's waving not drowning,

And it prefigures the undoing of hetero and homo both—perversion
    universal—the end of capital

    That was 1972

But the jokes are still funny—"No one ever threatens to take away
    your anus"—

And it does still feel like he got something right—

Male paranoia as a problem for us all

    *

33

I forget how easy it is to spot me

Traipsing by the slightly drunken Sunday morning park-bench
    cowboys with a quart of berries and my head in the clouds—

"Hey man, how was the market?"

    It was good—we share some berries—

And as I turn to go he says, "Dude, guess what?"

I pause. "If anyone tried to shoot you I would stop them."

    *

One of those berries was different

Popping it absently back at home I felt myself begin to float beside the
    window—

    I drifted down among the alders—

Then I was clambering through brush into a complicated nest of
    freeway ramps

They darkened shifting over me—Dark City, Piranesi prison—

It reached into my guts—I dropped to my knees—

And crouching there I vomited out a thick coagulate blood

The iron struts withdrew—before me was a broad and leveling path—

And there as though she'd been waiting was a silent, regal kari
    edwards—

Effortlessly upright in a feathered silver cape, her hair swept
    into coils

Meeting her gaze was like a cup of coffee—abruptly I wanted to chat—

kari! You should see the trans kids now—is it quiet there—has it really
    been ten years—

But she just extended her hand to pass me a cup—

OK a chalice—

Clearly designed to suit my dream life—it hefted like an unignited
    lightsaber, with an ice-blue pulse below the rim—

But I couldn't hold it for long—my hands were too substantial—

It sank into my groin

& there—right where normally I can only moan—

It made an opening in me—a gate so outward-facing passing through
   it felt like discomposing—

And all that night the demons I had thought were only ever sent to
   torment me—they swaddled me—

In silver sheets beside a high and open window—

And I slept

   *

You wake into the heavy world

The gunman enters the club with an AR15 of course, trailing 45
   Republican senators and the last round of the dead

They howl as the shooting begins—impotently urging dancers under
   tables, toward the exits—reaching for the falling bodies they
   can't touch—

Then they're gone

Your demons slam you down into the concrete on the corner of 26th
and Mission

*Now*, they howl—

Now your dream is over

\*

The final stanza of that Oppen poem is interesting

He writes, "indeed a poet's room / Is a boy's room / And I suppose
that women know it"

Then he concludes,

> "Perhaps the unbeautiful banker
> Is exciting to a woman, a man
> Not a boy gasping
> For breath over a girl's body"

So yeah poets are male

But also: boys are beautiful

And: women don't like boys    they like men who make them feel like
girls

Also: fuck bankers

And the whole perfume of ashamed resentment, I get that

I remember reading a passage in *The Book of Laughter and
Forgetting* when I was like 16 where a woman turns to
her lover and says, "You fuck like an intellectual"
and thinking yeah, that's gonna be me

But maybe most interesting—*breath*

I've always had this feeling that maybe all my sexual fantasies are
really just breathing exercises

Like you clench your body to release your diaphragm

Like you drop for a moment down into something only seemingly
abyssal

Down into matter, flux, the green world

Down into the immaterial sponginess that makes the bankers and the
    poets both go *unhhh*

\*

Hetero / Homo // Cis / Trans

Just as a matter of language?

    I'm not the same as myself

    I'm not the opposite of myself

I'm downstream from the values of some ancient warrior class that
    got to decide what men and women are

    Not that they knew they were doing it

I love that moment in *Billy on the Street* where the bros pounce
    on this cute boy in midtown Manhattan and they're like,
    "Dude: for a dollar: true or false: masculinity is a prison"—
and go apeshit high-fiving him when he smiles and says "true!"

    I crumple a little when it's clear that the answer to the
    question in the article I'm reading called "Is Masculinity
    a Death Cult" will quite persuasively be "yes"

I realize it's preposterous to pit my tiny life against the tidal swells of
    the history of gender,

    It's like scorning wealth—

But every day in graceful carriage I can see it all undone so easily,

If only we'd all undo it—

    *

Moods like waves of cortisol

How they leave me feeling hidebound, autoimmune—like will I only
    ever desire what I desire,

What kind of poet is that?

    I washed with the chemicals they gave me to wash with

    I felt with the feelings I was given to feel

Remember queer theory? How we used to joke our sexuality was
    "graduate student"?

I want my sexuality to be "courage"

I want that sweet reductio that pours out everything and leaves your
    demons agape

Then I'll let them come to me, shyly in a circle

Was it all so quick, they'll ask, like you were never even there?

In all that paranoia—did you ever even sense the ache of love?

Yes, I'll say, I saw the stars dissolving at the break of day

Yes     I heard the nightbird

# WHITE MEADOWS

*There are no meadows in the mind of the oppressed. There are only slums, factories, forced-labor fields, border detention facilities, Guantánamos, Abu Ghraibs, cops, devastated streets and jails.* —Heriberto Yépez

Or, as I remember reading it, "What is *up* with white poets and meadows?"

     \*

It's like there's a scrap of glory in me I was asked to keep safe while the world goes to hell.

Or like everyone has one.

Or like the world has always been hell.

Or like some parts are lovely because the other parts are hell.

I grew up in the suburbs of a lovely part.

     It was really just a housing tract—

Let's call it White Meadows—

But I grew up and wrote some poems.

I got a few sweet emails about them—

>   "I really like the pop culture and gay sex references in your
>   poetry"

They were poems about cities / poems about meadows / poems about
let's call it the global north.

>   But the slums and the suburbs—

All through the 80s and 90s I tried to fathom this

Finally it led me to the avant-garde

>   Whoops—

>   *

Was it always on analogy to speed?

But speed is just a fear suppressant—slow yourself down and it rushes
back in—

"Every time North Americans feel 'unsafe,' others get killed abroad.
    If there is something that North American critical agents need
    to learn, it is to feel 'unsafe'"

I see that I am frequently unsafe

    Unsafe to others—

But when I *feel* unsafe

    Which is kind of always—

It's not because I worry that a brown person's gonna steal my stuff

It's because the violence I grew up seeing, seeing and repressing—

    The violence done to black people, to brown people, to
        poor people, to women—

I never saw a guarantee that I would be spared the same

Of course you could say that every day of my life has been that
    guarantee

    Like who are you kidding white boy

But a child doesn't know that

So something worse happens—

You develop a fear of being brought into contact with the violated

Your very desire to help people becomes a barrier to knowing them,
    since you're afraid you couldn't offer actual solidarity—

And you probably couldn't

Of course this is narcissistic, like children are, and it factors out the
    courage and the buoyancy of the oppressed

But relying on an image of the courage of the oppressed is just a way
    to say godspeed and be done with them—

"Them"

Ethics, fuck

You can't think your way out of this

You can't feel your way out

You sure can't write your way

*

In the North American suburbs we used to ride our bikes around
    when school was out

It was hilly—there were nooks and hollows where adults would
    never go

You'd lay down your bike and—I don't know—make up stories—sing
    under your breath—

It had a lawless, world-receiving feel to it

I rarely felt normal but I remember being happy

    *

Heriberto I would have liked to ride bikes with you

But you were busy having the childhood that afforded mine

Maybe they made you waste your intellect on building some toy I
    played with mindlessly

Maybe you assembled my bicycle chain

Up here we were slowly becoming the Rust Belt

And you—

All those hits the peso took—just to help the coked-up,
    ravening dollar

You were becoming the avant-garde

        *


ANNUIT COEPTIS

*Aeneid* 9.625

The young Ascanius, inexperienced in battle, but hungry for glory

The full hexameter translates,

        "Omnipotent Jupiter, favor my audacity while I try to kill this
        kid"

Apollo rushes in for high fives once he's down and claps our hero on
    the shoulder

"And that, my boy, is the path to the stars"

Fast forward to the founding of Alba Longa

Also to every soldier who's ever told me I owe him for my
    "freedoms"—

    As opposed to owing my freedom to like 3 million slaves

Anyway Ascanius got his

There was nothing left of Alba Longa after the Romans got pissed off

Now it's a suburb


    *


This one

This cut peach on a table

This one, this cut peach, this is the one

    This is the one I will enjoy without believing I deserve it—

Good faith on credit / the North American dream

The history of dreams—and the childhood history of bumping into
the dream's back door—

The rejected awareness that your whole life was built, as
your parents' lives were, on the backs of others elsewhere—

And that your suffering while not less real for this did not in
the least exonerate you from supporting the design by
which an infinite misery was built up to cushion you—

The history of the dream's design—

That's the history of your becoming white—

\*

There's a corner of the UC Berkeley campus called the "Faculty
Glade"

I used to cross it sometimes, when I taught there, on my
way to Caffé Strada

It's not far from Sproul

In June I heard some music there designed to address the
"Anthropocene"

It was an interesting blend of drone sounds and the kinds of
flourishes in brass that spell inauguration

To me this meant it was a kind of sunrise song, but not for
any single sunrise

Anyway everybody listening was white

The musicians were arranged at the glade's perimeter, I think to give
the audience a comforting sense of being embraced by earth

White people picked their way contemplatively among the seated

And if you listened hard, beneath the drone sounds and the trumpet
flourishes you could hear the sounds of protest from 500 feet
away,

And that was the sound of the "Anthropocene":

Murder murder murder / peaceful droning

Listen I don't blame John Luther Adams for writing his terrestrial
music

I would like to see Alaska someday

But I have to say—

Against the backdrop of the agony in Sproul—all those
    contemplative expressions looked like signs of debility . . .


    *


Heriberto I imagine only history will tell me whether it's mine to
    recite the names of the murdered in my poems, when I didn't
    know them

       I don't want to make it worse

Many mediations separate me from the political dead

And I don't know how many separate you from yours

But if it's not mine to name them in whatever genre this is, I need to
    learn the contours of the genre in which I could,

Especially if it's not poetic—


    *

This past week in mid-July on the spongy floor of a meadow by the
    sea we scattered the ashes of Patrick Baroch

    He was a friend and a mystery to me

He had a technician's way of taking pains and a saboteur's talent for
    the mischievous

And lord he hated office work

He was a spangle in a box of buttons, if you know what I mean

He made a video of me once at Bedlam Coffee in Seattle reading
    "The Dial," which took fifteen minutes

        I tried to lose myself in the ambient sound, but they'd
            turned off the music—

        I tried to focus on his camera's little tripod,

        But I just got more self-conscious as I read—

        And when I got to the end he said, "Perfect! Now let's do it
            again."

Patty had a kind of boundless joy in him and he went through hell

What we scattered him into I don't know

The northern Pacific shone

It shone like infinite rail

It shone through all the sounds it made, and it made all sound

    It made the shorebirds cry

    It made the cypress creak

It made the sound of losing your companion

I wouldn't call Patty's a political death, though the Bush years ground
    him down

I couldn't tell you exactly how his whiteness was different from mine,
    just as his queerness was

And I don't know what it sounds like to the rest of the world when one
    white man remembers another

But I don't believe there's any purely white space—

The muses aren't all white thank god and they know the names of the
　　songs you played while you wrote your elegies


\*


So, Heriberto—

The internet tells me you plan to quit writing poems

I'm going to miss your mischief

I'm going to miss your underworlds, rotated 90 degrees

Those Homeric journeys where you have to sneak over walls

This summer on the Russian River I picked up a copy of Lorca
　　translations and came across a line toward the end of "Ode to
　　Walt Whitman" where he writes,

　　　"Una danza de muros agita las praderas,"

Sorry for my Spanish. Anyway I thought of you—or, I thought of us—
　　on either side of walled-in meadows

For Lorca Whitman is the right kind of faggot—manly, national

In this admiration he resembles nothing so much as half the gay men I
    know, but that's another poem

    When I think of their two deaths it breaks me

I have no illusions about hybridity—

I know no hybrid poetry can bridge the gap between the flowered
    procession and the unmarked grave

I know there's no right ratio between the peso and the dollar, any more
    than there's a fair price for a loaf of bread

Bread should be free

Children should flourish

    And I can't believe I have to say this—

Guantánamo should burn to the ground

Normally I'd add, and in its place let there spring up a *meadow*—

But I can almost hear you smack your forehead

It's not your job to find me a better ending,

Though you already have—

"History is not cyclical but its form is scroll-like"

Far-flung words and letters warped into relation—

Scrolls are full of wormholes

So I'm stripping this poem—not of rhetoric, of self,

But of its wish to end—

It cannot end—

It can only get smaller—

Small enough to worm from recto to verso

I'm down to one-line stanzas and a scrap of glory here

I'll see you on the other side

# THE SHORE

Then a wave rolled through us

Terrible buoyancy as I held your hand

Wave made out of voices, passing through our bodies by a fatal openness
   to sound

Thoughts unfinished on the flowered notepads—

In their wake a crunching thud

   *

The shore is the outline of the body of the sea

And the movement of its crashing is its aura

Whatever's stacked in us along our spines, what energy,

   The sea disperses, multiplies—

Its tidal swells, its reefs,

Even just its feather's pressure in the upper shallows—

It shapes us into bodily form

The sea surprises me

It reaches into human darkness—not with light but with salinity

*

Stevens called it "the pressure of reality"

Whitman wrote, "The dark threw its patches down upon me also"

The things you have to push against on late imperial streets—

Sharp tongues, defeated glances,

The whole taut net of the social order

Just once I would like to walk by that nail salon and see a white woman
giving a Vietnamese lady a pedicure

Make that a white guy

Make it for a century

And the president's man saying ooh scary, there has to be "darkness"
in power,

His stupid Gnosticism—

It's exhausting every morning to have to say No, there is not a war in
heaven

It's hard enough each day to care for one another without having to
wade through the leaflets they drop down on us

So you say it with your body, and your face—

You look a stranger in the eye, you're brushing off your shoulders,
and you say to each other without words,

What the fuck does *he* know about the dark?

*

Walk with me now through the warehouse district

Past the civic fountains and the reclaimed spaces,

Quote unquote,

Past the sidewalk cafés melodious laughter long-stemmed glasses

It's easy now to feel the rocking motion underneath the pavement

After years of study it's not hard to feel the movement of
    commodities,

To see the radiant city as a hellscape—

But I won't let the end of all my reading be becoming saturnine,

I worked too hard for that—

And anyway I saw the hellscape before I read the books

I saw it as a boy

The men who never put it into words—

I see it now in bodies and in gazes, every day

Resting cop face

Resting banker face

A hurt-girl face that's disappointed prettiness

And the guy who came up to my boy and pointed at me and said,
    "He's a faggot"—

The undoing jolt when we looked each other in the eye

So yes the city is a hellscape

But the death-pulse of commodities is just an imitation of the waves
    that pass through us—

Never forget that

They nudged us into life and through that pinhole death they'll draw
    us out to sea


\*


Release from the pressure of reality—

You feel that sometimes, right?

For me it's like the lead boots coming off

Those moments when I don't feel guilty or ashamed

The sudden freedom makes me feel prophetic and hilarious, walking
through the airport

Nope hate football sorry not so much with tanks no not impressed by
men on CNN

It gives me this quite healthy feeling of wanting to punch someone,
possibly a friend, in a sparring sort of way—

But then they call you to the gate

*

Travelers! I move among you with uncertain status

I wait while they call Diamond, Platinum, active military

I catch myself dreaming of a life where I'm just rich enough to harbor
everyone around me, has it come to that?

I try to imagine the abolition of the value-form but I come up empty-
handed

I can see Yosemites uncounted underneath Antarctic ice

I can hear a neolithic sound, a cave going Om for twenty
thousand years

I see how I'm the whale, and how the whale is me

But what's on the other side? Nada

Just because I have tremendous faith in people doesn't mean I think
we're going to win

The rich have their guns and their data mining

But I know a dozen teenagers with better politics than Auden

Poor Auden! Always getting beaten up on the left

OK better politics than Hugh MacDiarmid

Those kids—more queer, less Leninist, more kind—

Better students of capital—

I hope I make a decent uncle

*

In the great transition I think it'll be the nurses not the doctors

The nuns and not the priests

Will there be retirees who never gave a shit?

Interns who don't?

Soldiers who were only ever in it for the scholarships

I'm having these thoughts where I always do, in a café window seat

I've got this effortful mildness on my face meant to counteract the
    low-level intra-bourgeois competitiveness in which all
    middle-class children are trained . . .

Will the drivers who supply the Whole Foods?

Will the EMTs?

I feel like most of us would help each other since so few of us are
    actually profiting from this state of affairs

I know I'm not

And I've been paid to keep it going—

*

People don't come from much

Mine don't, at least

A gloving factory / some lawn equipment

They're made from scratch

Easy to destroy

And the palmlike pressure keeping them together—

It feels like you would get the bends from even just the tiniest evasion
of how we've been embodied

But there are dreams that pulse into the morning after with the
brightness of relief from speciation

And other gravities in which the stars fall straight down like a drip

Halfway up a hill from the Pacific in the early light today instead of
        just a man I saw like flecks of mica in the molding of a handsome
        face the sea—

I don't mean metaphorically, I don't mean literally,

        I mean an opening in me

        I felt the body of the ocean, and the shore

I felt a deepest flexion in my hips,

        Like a launch from out of the void—

My son—

        I felt you mimic it

There was no shore, and you and I were swimming.

# LAST GLIMPSE

Then I gave it up

I gave up thinking that the song I heard was the song of the world

I gave up lyric, gave up reverie, I gave up aesthesis—

I left my notebook on the park bench open with its pages riffling

I kept my head down

I said OK fine Elon Musk is the most important person on the planet

I did not read "Ozymandias"

But like that monument I started to crumble

Down I fell, down into earth, down into its deep revising heat—

And on the other side, my life's antipode—

Everything just slightly realigned

A hesitation in the driverless cars

A hint of lemon in the eucalyptus

Also absence—

A shimmer in the air where epic had been

A little grave of daffodils around the first-person
pronoun

Quiet but not silent—a pitter in the canopy—

You look down at your impression in the grass and go oh, so that's why
we sleep on our sides . . .

You no longer need to know the end of the story

You no longer dread the great devaluation

No ziggurats collapsing

No cities on a plain

You shake yourself, head high like a horse,

And step out into all the rain that's ever rained.

\*

Saba—the light these summer nights—

It thins the line between not-here and here

It lifts the ceiling on the sky

Those higher presences—like traffic cops they feign indifference

But they feed on life's detail—they need our beating hearts—

The redbud, the myrtle

They make a gate—you might get anything—

Some package from Amazon

Some Galadriel come up the walk

At 7 pm with life and busyness around you and the spectrum pulsing in the background you're like dude you need to run some language over this shit because it's beautiful

Then you do the dishes

Later at 3 am your dream life punts the excess back to waking

consciousness, saying *you* take care of it

Effects, perfumes—

The purple flower of the Russian sage

The silvered surface of the stoop

And all the friends who've swirled around it summer nights—

Here—not here—

I merge onto the far right lane to find you

*

What was your life? What is mine?

I have only very awkward ways of writing biographically

These two eager boys—

One's an opera singer—one does something he calls "energy law"—

They have the same shoes

Maybe I'm watching the beginning of their life together

Maybe I'm just watching the class reproduce itself

Laughter, gesture, nervous self-extension—

You hope it opens onto something

You hope they won't be cruel

Watcher! Geometer! Try it on yourself why don't you

All those years I thought I was a poet and I was just some person on
the metro

But I'm OK with being numerable . . .

Number of beats, number of breaths—

Each of us pulsing through the nights—each a portion of the sources
of plenty—

The chanson de geste of your hand across the page

The troubadour amour of your eyes on the horizon

And the voice in my head that speaks to me like I'm a child—

Some days I'm like shut up superego

Some days I just say, please always speak to me this way

    *

Relaxing on the shore that won't be here in 50 years

    Sea-foam on the sea-wall

Swallows tilting on their swallow-house

In times of despair it is customary for the poet to project himself
    onto some animal life imagined as freer—

        I have a theory that the further the projection the worse the
        situation

        Reversing the equation you get, hey 2019, what's it like to
        be a slime mold?

But life distracts me—

Child-things in the yard—the hula-hoops and bottles of bubbles—

Single-use plastic that Allison will track—

If I were Rick I'd use this bit of poem to orient myself—

    Lumpy couch on screened-in porch diagonal to the wind—the
    buoys, the birds—the pleasure craft—and north-northwest the
    domes of the Air Force base housing what—

My poetry can't do what Rick's and Allison's can, though it's partly for
    them—

    Shoes tossed crosswise on the kitchen floor

    Sleeves of jackets inside out

And the Air Force base is a Navy base—or, it's the Naval Air Systems
    Command base

    Military websites are very strange

TOP NEWS has Gerald Ford announcing "the future of carrier aviation"

And there's a button at the bottom with a flotation device and a hotline
    number that says "life is worth living"

Back on the porch I've just finished reading "Sea Surface Full of
  Clouds" to Mateo

I said something garbled and academic afterward but I think he liked it

There's this rocking tandem in the poem between the shifts in what
  the color of the water's likened to, and the shifting of the color of
  the water

It has this metaphysics where the substance of the world is light—
  where light leaves residues that become the things we know and
  keeps surpassing them—

Like capital! I think, because I'm that kind of intellectual—

The child in me asks, how does it move? And the older child says,

It moves like tilting swallows—like the osprey—like the bill of the
  heron, still, until . . .

    The adult keeps his mouth shut

But capital's not predation—your predator wants to *eat* you—

Capital wants your life—and if you get in its way it wants you dead

No—more than that—

It wants you to think you deserve to die

       \*

Red—a wave rolled through and gave us red—

       The ruby the cardinal the furnace—the bellows, the bull

A yellow like the sun at 7

       Like the wily seed of the grapefruit, which I chase around the
       room

The green ecliptic feel of everything that moves into position—

And violet—the moss of it—

I'm lying on my back in a flyover state, being flown over

Amiably bopping to apocalyptic Mormon pop

       Its braggadocio—

There's gonna be a lot of fronting about "the apocalypse" between now
    and the apocalypse

    White light—braggadocio—

After all these years a certain kind of man's body, passing by, still draws
    me in like a wormhole I can never make it to the other side of

    I wince from the too much citrus of it

Sometimes I startle myself—how can you still be so naïve?

I'm embarrassed some young part of me really thought, if you strain to
    look like a marine maybe all the young marines will fall for your
    antimilitarism

I'm dismayed that the default setting for "gay white guy" somehow
    remains "petty bourgeois"

    High-value bodies—low-value bodies—

You fight to keep un-seeing that—you say it's only virtual—

    But the real feeds on the virtual—

*

They put the goggles on you and you pop into a predawn Sonoran
   Desert

Orange becoming yellow at the rim—still deep purple toward the
   zenith

You're placed ambiguously among a group of maybe thirteen people

You've got a backpack on and they removed your shoes so it feels a
   little like an actual border crossing

The bodies are realistic but the state of the technology still means no
   one looks you in the eye

You know that thought experiment, what would you do if you were
   invisible,

      I think it comes from Plato?

You learn a lot about yourself when you actually are

For a second I thought I'd wedge myself between the CBP and the
   child, but the child had a mother

I'd never stood so close to a cop—we were chest to chest, me against
　　his vest, my eyes on his dead gaze—

Then I was inside him—the code allowed me in for three or four
　　seconds at a time—ribs and intercostals and a thumping heart,
　　with no surrounding tissue—

　　　　It would shove me out and I'd step back in

Fuck you, I'd mutter, and the interns would tug on my backpack

When the goggles came off I saw my feet had made a little check
　　mark in the sand, smeared where the tubing connected to its
　　power source

There was a "post-experience" lounge with a handsome young man
　　serving single-origin coffee

　　　　Enfleshed again—avenger no more—jotting hurried notes
　　　　　for my
　　　　single-person, paper-thin art

Someday when we storm the detention facilities I won't care about
　　that hierarchy

Sonnet, cinema, first-person shooter—

And in the terror of the walls all coming down, you know what, Saba?

We will never be afraid again

*

Summer nights—dark energy—

You have to be quiet to hear it

Somehow at dusk the little words from other languages become more
visible to me

Words on hinges, words on locks—

Dear friend—now you know better than I do—

I've been calling it death as though it hated me

But that's different from the dark involved with life

How happy our enemies must be to think we think we deserve to die—

And what a horrible year it's been

But death—I reached out my hand tonight and touched it, did you feel?

The fireflies—the fleur-de-lis—

All this time I've been ashamed for thinking what I hunger for is what
they want from me

I didn't know—

I didn't know I was so alive—

# ACKNOWLEDGMENTS

I would like to thank the editors of the following press and journals, in which versions or parts of some of these poems appeared:

Commune Editions: "The Victorious Ones"

*PEN Poetry Series* from PEN America: "You Surround Me"

*Boston Review*: "White Meadows"

*Almost Island*: "The Shore"

*Harper's*: "Last Glimpse," published as "A Dream"

"The Shore" is for Lissa Wolsak; "Last Glimpse" is for Saba Mahmood.